ACTIVE LISTENING

Understand People's Emotions and Thoughts to Avoid Conflict and Develop Deep Relationships (2022 Guide for Beginners)

Vincent Slater

CONTENTS

INTRODUCTION

Listening is an important skill that we must cultivate to be effective leaders and communicators. Active listening entails being aware of your thoughts as well as those of the other person. It entails not only hearing what they are saying but also seeing and feeling it in your mind's eye.

Active listening is the process of paying attention to what another person is saying and expressing interest in them or their concerns. It entails listening with your mind, eyes, and heart as well as your ears. You are actively attempting to understand the other person's point of view by observing both verbal and nonverbal cues such as body language or tone of voice.

A good listener detects cues from the other person that indicate what they want to say. A good listener will reflect the other person what they have heard so that the speaker knows they have been understood.

Active listening necessitates the removal of all other distractions to concentrate on what the speaker has to say. The listener must be completely unaware of time passing, their surroundings, or even their thoughts. When you are truly attentively listening, your mind is completely focused on the speaker. You will listen to what they have to say and try to understand where they are coming from.

Listening entails being aware of the emotions of the other person. It also entails projecting an image of comprehension while not being unduly influenced by their mood. When you are truly listening, you will want to reflect on what you have heard so that the speaker feels fully understood.

Active listening can be learned and developed into a skill that is useful in all aspects of life, including work and business, as well as personal relationships with friends, family, and partners.

Being an active listener allows us to see situations from another person's perspective.

Active listening is a skill that great leaders and communicators have mastered. There is no doubt that they will be extremely successful in their chosen field – in addition to understanding other people's thoughts and feelings.

Active listening is a skill that all of us must learn to be good listeners and communicators. The ability to listen well not only aids in the development of communication skills but also allows us to understand other people and their points of view.

Understanding people's points of view and listening to them is an important step toward developing mutual relationships, which are essential for success in any field.

We can learn a lot from how others communicate with us.
There are many different types of listening styles, which are often influenced by how we were raised as children. Sometimes our listening habits can wreak havoc on our relationships with others. We must adapt and change them to be successful. Everyone is different and listens in their way, but by being aware of these differences, you can improve your overall communication skills.
Listening is more than just hearing what we hear; it is also about comprehending the message behind the words. Listening is not a passive activity; it is an active process in which we concentrate all of our senses on what the speaker is saying and how they are feeling.

When we listen in this manner, our brains recognize patterns and distinguish between what we hear. This information can be used to respond appropriately to different speakers in various situations.

To be a good listener, we must be able to focus on what others are saying. We can accomplish this by becoming aware of how we process information in our brains. Our brains have a limited attention span and can only focus on one person talking at a time. When people speak, our short-term memory stores the speaker's words for a limited amount of time before asking us to repeat them. This is known as confirmation bias, and it assists us in processing what has been said. A good listener will recognize and correct what they hear. A bad listener will only hear what they want to hear and will not listen to the facts. Anxious people are more concerned with their fears and misunderstandings than with the speaker's concerns.

From work to family life, being a good listener is essential in all social situations. For example, when people are speaking, we can choose to be close to them and on the same wavelength, or we can stand back and offer a more detached opinion. Being a good listener may be difficult for us when we are having difficulty concentrating on what is being said. When someone is dealing with personal issues, they need to hear other people's perspectives as well as their own. Being a good listener not only ensures that they receive this information, but also helps them better understand themselves.

The art of listening is crucial, and the more we learn about it, the better we will be able to understand what others are thinking.

Our ability to listen is the true art of communication. Only by truly listening to one another can we be certain that the information passed on from one person to the next is accurate and truthful.

We must learn not only how to concentrate, but also how to be silent within ourselves, to listen effectively.

Active listening fosters understanding and empathy between two people. When we actively listen, the speaker has our full attention and understands that we are interested in what they have to say.

CHAPTER 1
WHY DO WE NEED TO LEARN HOW TO LISTEN?

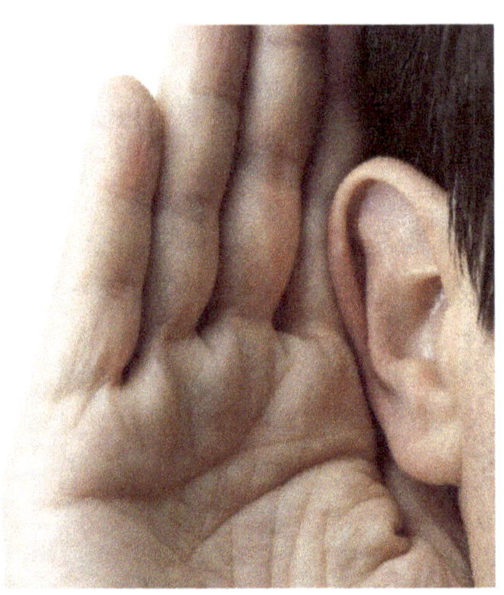

Listening entails much more than just hearing the sounds of other people's words. It necessitates paying attention not only to what someone says but also to their body language and tone of voice. It necessitates being fully present to comprehend what is going on in the other person's life.

Learning to listen not only assists us in better understanding the other person, but it can also assist us in listening to our inner voice. When we learn to listen, we open ourselves up to receiving information, wisdom, and guidance.

When two people are conversing, listening is most effective. Because the amount of information that can be exchanged in two-way communication is limited, listening as a separate skill plays an important role.

Listening is a two-way street. It entails not only hearing but also empathizing with the other person's needs, desires, and issues. When you are truly listening to someone, you will feel engaged and drawn in, as if they are speaking to your thoughts or feelings.

When you listen attentively, you are taking the time to hear and understand what the other person is saying.

Listening involves both nonverbal and verbal cues. Gestures, facial expressions, tone of voice, and posture are examples of nonverbal cues. Speaking slower and more clearly, reflecting on what the other person said when they pause in their conversation or asking clarifying questions about what they just said are all examples of verbal cues. Active listening is a way of demonstrating that you are actively participating in the conversation. Active listening also aids in the establishment of trust because people recognize your sincerity. As a result, they will feel more at ease discussing their thoughts and feelings with you.

Active listening enables you to respond in ways that demonstrate your comprehension. It improves communication by demonstrating that you are interested in what the other person has to say. It also helps to avoid miscommunication because misunderstandings are frequently caused by people believing they understand a message when they do not.

Effective communication necessitates active listening. It is the process of paying close attention to someone and comprehending what they are saying. When verbal communication fails to provide the information required, people turn to nonverbal cues such as gestures, facial expressions, and body language. For example, if a person does not feel heard, they will become defensive and eventually leave frustrated.

You can listen with your ears, with your eyes, or with both. You can use your body language to show that you are fully engaged in the conversation and understand what the other person is saying.

Active listening can be practiced in a variety of ways. You could listen to someone talking about one of their problems and ask questions to encourage them to share more information with you so that you can truly participate in the conversation. You may listen to someone's ideas on an important issue, but you may disagree with them. However, you can demonstrate that you are paying attention to their point of view by asking clarifying questions. For example, someone may be opposed to a new smoking ban in public places while you are in favor of it, but by inquiring as to why they are opposed to the new law, you can demonstrate your interest in their concerns and opinions.

Active listening allows us to see the other side of an argument so that we can better understand our own. This can assist us in communicating more effectively and providing others with the support they require to feel heard. Active listening also boosts our self-esteem.

According to studies, people who actively listen are more assertive and are perceived as more attractive and likable by others. People who actively listen are perceived to be more competent, which increases their credibility with others. Active listening is a critical skill that everyone must learn if relationships are to be productive, satisfying, and healthy. It is the most fundamental component of all relationships. Active listening is one of the most effective ways to improve interpersonal relationships. It's a powerful way of connecting with and relating to others. In all of our close relationships, we can use active listening to improve relationship satisfaction and reduce conflict. Active listening makes us more authentic, which leads to more positive interactions with others. We help others feel heard, understood, and loved when we actively listen.

Reasons for our inability to listen to others

Listening is a skill that can be honed and improved. It is a valuable asset for success in any aspect of life, especially those that require us to interact with others. We are not born with the ability to listen well, and it takes time and practice to improve.

Here are some of the reasons why we don't listen to others:
1. We've never been taught to listen.
   We may believe that listening is a skill that can be learned in school, but the classroom has rarely provided the necessary tools and techniques to learn it.
   To recognize other people's emotions or understand what they are attempting to express, we must observe what is said both directly and indirectly, without making any judgmental comments or suggestions (the difference between listening and doing).

2. We are unconcerned about what the other person has to say. This attitude is usually caused by a large number of voices we hear every day: television, radio, cell phone conversations, and so on. Although we do not always directly participate in these voices, they have an impact on how we treat and value the voices or opinions of others.

3. We are unaware of what is going on around us.
   It can be difficult to recognize when our prejudices, fears, or anxieties are interfering with our ability to listen. We might not be aware of our emotional reactions. It is critical to pause during an interaction to consider what we are reacting to and how it may be affecting our ability to communicate effectively.

4. Our attention is diverted by something else (unconsciously). The person speaks, but our minds are elsewhere. This is one of the reasons why we may not fully comprehend what is being said. We can only hear the words but do not understand what they mean. This is why different people can have different interpretations of the same words.
5. We are not aware of tone or body language.
   We will never be able to figure out what someone else truly

wants or feels unless we understand these things, which leads to a very limited understanding of the entire situation.

6. We are not hearing the entire message.
    We can get so caught up in what someone else is saying that we fail to hear what the person is trying to say. We may hear only a portion of it and then make a judgmental comment or two, which may completely blind us to the other person's intention or meaning.

7. We do not allow the other person to finish.
    Sometimes we have preconceived notions about what the other person is saying without allowing him or her to fully explain it. If we do not allow the person to finish, we may end up with a distorted understanding of what he is attempting to convey.

8. We anticipate how the other person will respond.
    We may persuade ourselves that having certain expectations is a good idea because we want to feel good about ourselves, but this will only discourage us from properly listening to another person's opinion or experience. This is not only incorrect because it leads to a very limited view of the entire subject, but the consequences could be quite damaging to our relationships.

9. We fail to remain present and allow the other person's experience and feelings to fully enter our minds.
    We may not realize it at times, but we are so preoccupied with what is going on around us that we are unable to focus on just one voice.

10. The noise of our thoughts and feelings distracts us.

All of these factors contribute to a poor listening experience, which can keep us from truly learning and understanding another person's intention or point of view, potentially affecting our relationship with that person as well as other people in our lives.

These are the ten most common ways that we fail to truly listen to others, and it's critical to be aware of these points to gain a better understanding of the concept of listening as a whole. This will also serve as a good foundation for us to build on as we learn how to improve our listening skills daily.

CHAPTER 2
THE DIFFERENT TYPES OF LISTENING

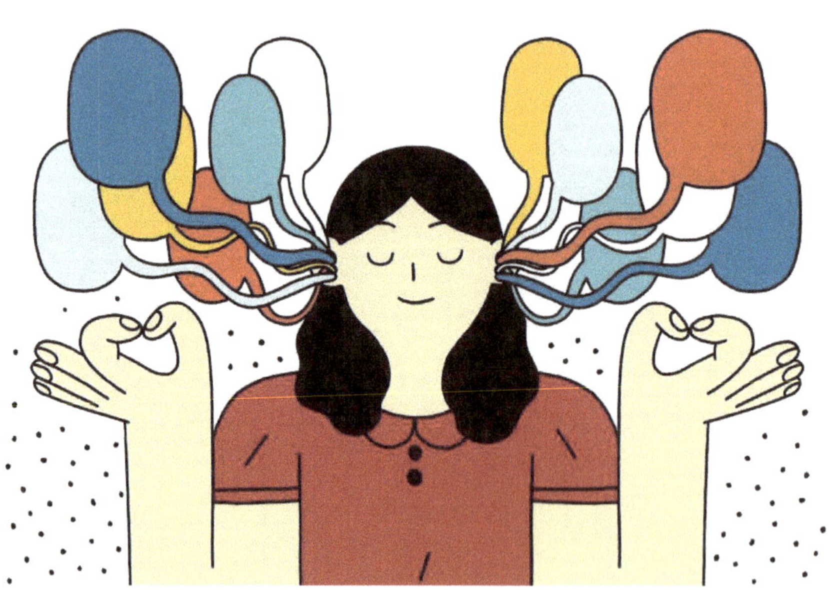

There are several ways to listen to someone, and each one serves a different purpose.

These are the various types of listening:

Thank you for listening.
This type of listening is the most effective way to comprehend what someone is saying without making incorrect assumptions. It increases your chances of understanding what you're hearing. It can be exhausting, however, because it requires your undivided attention.

The goal of appreciative listening is to understand what the speaker truly means rather than correcting grammar or other mistakes the speaker makes while speaking. You can jot down key points as you hear them if you're taking notes. This will allow you to concentrate on what the speaker is saying.

Maintaining a positive attitude aids the process by allowing you to listen more intently. It also allows you to feel empathy for the speaker, which will help you understand the message better. The more open-minded you are, the easier it will be to understand and appreciate what is said to you.

Listening with empathy
This type of listening is ideal for those who want to make others feel understood. It entails listening to what someone has said while attempting to put yourself in their shoes.
This type of listening allows you to show someone that you understand their emotions.

Listening to that is synthesized
Synthesized listening occurs when we take the initiative to conduct our research on a topic raised in conversation and then report our findings back to the other person. This is an excellent way to put your listening skills to use.

Synthesized listening
It allows you to provide useful information to someone while also encouraging them to develop their knowledge, ideas, and thoughts. It's also a good way to expand your knowledge in a specific field. The best way to do this is to spend some time researching a topic

thoroughly before engaging in a conversation about it. Then, if you notice them discussing something that piques your interest, let them know you can find out more about it for them if they are interested. This is a very effective method of communication. The more you know, the better you will be at listening to and understanding others.

If you take the initiative and ask questions about the topic at hand, you will be able to get more out of what they have to say. These can include questions about the subject, when they began learning about it, who they learned it from, how they feel about what they were learning, and why.

The disadvantage of synthesized listening is that it is more difficult to engage others in conversation than simply taking notes. It essentially necessitates more effort on your part. Some people may also be hesitant to assist someone else in learning about a topic if they are not already familiar with it.

Listening critically
Critical listening is used to absorb information more critically and is most commonly used when people are attempting to evaluate or assess something. It's ideal for people who want to base their decisions on what they've learned from listening.

When you want to call out someone who is making factual errors or getting their facts wrong, critical listening can come in handy. Critical listeners do more than just listen; they also observe and pay attention to details that might have slipped past them if they weren't paying attention. The distinction between critical and active listening is that critical listening is used to take notes and collect information that can be used to make a decision or some form of judgment, whereas active listening is used to absorb information.

Analytical hearing
Analytical listeners are often good researchers, and they can put their skills to use when looking for information on a specific topic or subject matter. They can see things that others may not be able to see because they are looking at them from a different perspective.

Analytical listening is ideal for people who want to base their decisions on information they have gathered and analyzed. Someone with an analytical ear can pick up on messages and nuances that others may miss. This type of listening is also beneficial for people who are open-minded and want to understand new perspectives.

Analytical listening is ideal for understanding complex issues, organizations, or people. Analytical listeners pay close attention to the information given to them and use it to draw their conclusions and make decisions based on their findings. This type of listener is also skilled at analyzing data and determining whether something is true or false in a given situation.

Analytical listening is also beneficial for researchers who must actively use the data they collect daily. Analytical listeners can also be good at staying focused and avoiding distractions that others may notice.

Analytical listeners can be excellent problem solvers because they can comprehend complex issues and provide clear solutions.

They can determine what is causing the problems and what needs to be done to fix them by analyzing the problems from all angles.

Analytical listeners use all available information to determine what is and are not relevant, such as a person's tone of voice, tonal inflections, facial expressions, or body language. This type of listening assists them in determining what is going on with the other person and how it can help them better understand the situation.

Analytical listeners always make certain that they have all of the information they require to make sound decisions. They bring logic to any situation and can see things from multiple perspectives, which is why they are good at devising creative solutions to complex problems.

Because of their ability to analyze the world around them, they frequently find themselves in positions of leadership and other responsibility.

Listening in both directions

Reciprocal listening is a two-way communication method in which both listeners and speakers participate in the conversation. The speaker discusses something in their mind, and the listener attempts to understand what they are saying by paraphrasing or asking questions about what they are discussing.

When it's your turn to speak, make sure you're not interrupting the other person verbally; you can do this by pausing before you speak. If you feel you're moving too quickly, try pausing and taking a deep breath. This can help to break up a conversation and defuse tension. If the listener does not understand something, they can engage in reciprocal listening by paraphrasing and asking questions. When the listener engages in reciprocal talking, the speaker feels understood and can express themselves more freely.

While it is beneficial to discuss a topic that is of interest to you, it is critical to remember to listen to the other person and refrain from lecturing them. This can be difficult, but understanding why they feel the way they do will give you a much better understanding of the person in front of you. If you have too many questions and not enough time, see if there is another time you could meet for a longer conversation.

Listening passively

When you listen passively, you are not actively participating in a conversation. Instead, you simply listen to what the speaker says.

Passive listening does not require much energy or focus, but it does necessitate caution and sensitivity. It is best not to interrupt or ask questions when passively listening.

When you listen passively, you avoid taking control of the conversation, which can lead to greater understanding and engagement. This type of listening is essential for anxious people because it allows the speaker to narrate without the other person worrying about what they are saying.

The listener should refrain from interfering with the speaker. If a pause occurs during a monologue, it is best not to jump in with irrelevant information. This can be avoided by being aware of when it occurs and giving the other person enough time to continue uninterrupted.

Here are some practical things to think about when passively listening:
- Your goal should be to observe rather than to explain.
- Be mindful of how frequently you speak and how frequently you interrupt others.
- Try not to speak at all.
- Try not to be judgmental. It is preferable to reflect on what you are hearing rather than make comments that could spark an argument or offend the speaker.
- Be honest with yourself and your feelings. Allow yourself to be open without attempting to control or influence the conversation.

Listening actively

Active listening enables collaboration during communication, which is where an ideal level of communication occurs. Listeners must actively participate in the conversation for understanding to occur. When you listen in this manner, you are not distracted by other thoughts or ideas that may come to mind. For example, while the speaker is speaking, one may listen well but have their thoughts. Active listening also allows for the clarification of terminology and concepts, as well as the gathering of additional information from speakers.

Active listening allows the speaker to receive feedback, which is necessary for the other person to better understand their message. This is critical for both the speaker and the listener. The speaker may require clarification on their message, or they may be accustomed to receiving feedback from others during a conversation.

It can be confusing and stressful for people who are not used to receiving feedback.

Active listening necessitates paying attention at all times and not rushing through a conversation. While listening to others, it is important to maintain eye contact, avoid interrupting the speaker, and listen for keywords or phrases that may be part of what they are trying to say. Consideration of the information presented by the speaker necessitates focus.

Active listening is the most effective mode of communication. It enables better understanding and relationship strengthening. It is also beneficial to observe both verbal and nonverbal messages conveyed during the interaction. Active listening skills can be enhanced by practicing five key skills: attending, reflecting, clarifying, questioning, and summarizing.

CHAPTER 3:
BEFORE LISTENING, WORK ON YOURSELF

To actively listen, the first thing you must do is be present.

To fully hear and understand what is being said, your mind must be free of all distractions. When listening, your body must be in a state of energetic stillness: This includes no texting or putting yourself in a stressful or demanding situation, such as a board meeting. People tend to speak more openly when they have someone's undivided attention because they are less concerned about their words being misconstrued or appearing rude. When you are in an energetic state of stillness, you can listen and respond much more easily.

Listen with your ears rather than your mind.
When people speak to you, they are communicating with you through their words. However, most people listen with their minds rather than their ears, relying on their intellect and past experiences to determine what the other person is saying. To truly hear another person's words, you must "listen with your ears." Stop worrying about what you're going to say next or what you have to do at work. Simply listen to what is being said without questioning it. When you listen with your ears rather than your intellect, you will be able to understand and respond much more easily.

After you've finished listening, become receptive.
When you have fully comprehended what has been said to you, you must become receptive. You must now actively listen rather than simply hearing the words. You must also allow your body and mind to be receptive for this to happen. Simply relax your body so that there are no more muscular tense reactions to talking or being in the presence of other people.

Be open within yourself, then listen intently. The ability to actively listen and truly hear what the other person is saying takes practice but can become second nature once you've mastered it. It will have been worthwhile when you cannot only hear, but also understand what others are saying and respond appropriately.

Your conversations will be more rewarding and interesting as a result.

You will not always agree with others, but actively listening will help you respond with greater understanding and respect.

Consider why you're in the room when you're having a conversation.

When you're in a conversation, your main goal is to be present.

Being present entails listening and being open to hearing what the other person has to say. If you are only observing or considering what to say next, you are not truly present because you are disconnected from the conversation.

By being receptive, you can be present with your thoughts while also being open to hearing what others have to say.

When you are fully present and open, you will be able to understand and assist in any way that is required.

Don't act like a "know-it-all."

The worst thing that can happen during a conversation is for one person to try to appear to be a know-it-all. They attempt to present a point of view that is always correct and superior to others.

Because they are not taking the time to listen to others' points of view, they appear rude or inconsiderate.

It is perfectly acceptable to ask questions if someone else has a different point of view or wants you to understand what they're saying. But, when someone tells you something, don't try to figure out how they're wrong. As much as you can, listen and comprehend. This is the only way you will truly develop as a listener and caretaker.

When someone tries to tell you something they believe you should know, treat their words and ideas with respect. Be open to new experiences by listening to people from various backgrounds and attempting to see different points of view.

Many times, when you think someone is wrong, they are correct. Understandably, you would disagree in that case.

Be open-minded and try to find the best solution possible, because arguments rarely solve problems. It's important to solve problems with kindness; there's no point arguing about things that don't matter in the long run. You may have to spend a long time correcting yourself if you are too far in the wrong. This is not an easy task and can be very exhausting. As a result, don't argue for the sake of arguing.

Be astute but not arrogant. Don't think you're smarter than the other person or that he or she is stupid; sometimes they just don't know what you know.

Instead of being present and listening to understand what the other person is saying, we are frequently trying to prove ourselves right.

When we can truly listen and understand, we can assist in any way that is required.

This will enable us to become good listeners, as well as open-minded, compassionate, and caring individuals who care about others.

Your friends and family are aware of the true you.

They know who you are because they have been paying attention to you.

They've been doing their job as your friends and family for a long time by actively listening to what you have to say.

Active listening is an effective communication skill that can result in positive outcomes on both sides of the equation.

Active listening is a communication skill with counseling roots, but it is also a life skill that anyone can benefit from.

When we actively listen to another person, we are communicating to them on some level what they need to know. We are demonstrating our concern for them and making them feel heard.

Active listening is a skill that is highly valued in relationships because it can aid in the maintenance of a healthy relationship. We tend to be more passive when communicating with others, whether through conversation or in writing. We tend to speak rather than listen, which can be harmful to our relationships. However, this does not imply that you should become overbearing in your communication while attempting to actively listen!

Active listening is an excellent way to strengthen and deepen your interpersonal relationships. It can help you truly understand them, what they are going through, and how you can best assist them.

We are actively listening if we are taking in their words and their message. We are not simply waiting for our turn to speak. Active listening entails being completely engaged with the person with whom we are communicating rather than simply waiting our turn.

Although active listening is not a passive act, we are only giving the other person our full attention. We are actively listening to them and informing them that their voices have been heard.

Communication is essential in all types of relationships, and the ability to actively listen will only strengthen the relationship. When you listen to someone, you are indicating to them that they can talk to you about anything. They can be completely honest with you, and their problems will not be dismissed.

We show the other person that they are important by actively listening to them. We demonstrate that we care about them and are willing to listen to them. In this way, we can contribute to the development of trust in a relationship.

Good listening skills can help you improve your relationships with those around you. Relationships require nurturing over time.

Methods for Recognizing If You Aren't a Good Listener and How to Improve

You may feel that you are not a good listener at times, that you speak too much or that you do not acknowledge what the other person is saying. You will learn if you are a good listener and how to improve your listening skills by reading this section.

To begin, if you are conversing with someone else and at some point, during the conversation, you start thinking about something unrelated to the conversation, this could be a sign that you are not a good listener. Second, if you find yourself listening solely to gain attention or approval from others, this could indicate that you are not a good listener.

Third, if you find yourself using the words of others to fill in gaps in your speech or thoughts, you are probably not a good listener. Finally, if you are having difficulty understanding what others are saying, this could be a sign.

There are numerous approaches to becoming a good listener. It takes time and effort to develop good listening skills, just like any other skill. Most people never learn how to listen effectively.

They are so preoccupied with what they are going to say next that they miss most of what the person is saying right now.

The first step toward becoming a better listener is becoming aware of our listening habits. We become aware by observing how we react when others speak to us and by soliciting feedback from others.

When we begin to listen to ourselves, we become aware of our communication habits, asking ourselves where we are not listening and what we are doing while listening.

Paying attention to your body language while listening is one way to improve your listening skills. You may be able to notice how active or passive you are in your listening by doing so. Examine yourself to see if you are leaning forward while listening or backward like a turtle with his shell closed when someone speaks.

Another way to improve your listening skills is to remember that when someone speaks, they have specific needs that must be met, and your needs should not be the first thing on their list. For example, if someone is speaking to you about something important and you keep interrupting with your remarks, this could indicate that you are not a good listener.

It is critical to keep the person speaking with you in mind while you are listening. It's critical to understand what they're trying to say and why they're saying it. It is critical to understand not only what someone is saying to you, but also what they are not saying. It is critical to consider why someone is speaking with you and what they expect from you.

Professional communication entails listening, comprehending what others are saying, and providing feedback in a way that the other person will understand.

Being able to accurately hear what someone is saying to you is the most difficult aspect of being a good listener. It implies that you must do your best to concentrate on the conversation at hand. If you become distracted while listening to someone, you will miss what they are trying to say to you.

It is critical to be able to listen and pay attention to avoid missing important information. It is critical to consider what you are hearing and then accurately communicate that to the person with whom you are conversing.

CHAPTER 4
THE LISTENING PROCESS

The process by which a participant perceives information is known as listening.

When we hear something, it travels from our ears to our brain, where it is processed and stored. Listening can also refer to our awareness of what is happening around us in general or within a specific activity.

Listening is one of the primary ways in which humans learn to communicate. The hearing provides information about the physical environment, while listening provides information about other people. A listener has two objectives: first, to accurately perceive the speaker's ideas (i.e., what they're saying), and second, to communicate their understanding of the speaker's ideas.

The brain controls the process of hearing and understanding speech in a series of steps:

The message has been received.

The physical component of the massage stimulates sensory receptors and is transmitted via the auditory pathway. The auditory system includes sound receptors in the ears known as the outer, middle, and inner ear, which play an important role in hearing and interpreting speech.

The auditory system's messages are then transmitted to the brain via nerves that transmit electrical impulses. The auditory cortex receives signals that are processed by millions of nerve cells to form perceptions or images of sounds. This process is what allows us to hear the voice of another person.

When we listen to a sound, however, there are many more complex factors to consider, such as the position of the head and which ear is stimulated.

What we hear is an impression of the signal as it is processed in real-time by our auditory system.

Message processing or interpretation
The message is analyzed to process or identify its component sounds. These processes will either combinc aspects of similar sounds into a unified concept or provide individual identities to separate words. Speech is associated with several responses, including comprehension and memory, which listeners use to understand what they hear. It entails the ability to recognize and comprehend the speaker's intent, as well as to identify the words that are being spoken. Listeners must be able to interpret words and the intent behind them to accomplish this. After that, the message is decoded into a series of mental images or concepts.

The message is understood by the listener in terms of his or her personal past experiences (worldview) and mental models. During this stage, the majority of active listening occurs.

In response to the message
The listener contributes his or her thoughts to the message. This works best when the listener can summarize what they've heard and the speaker understands and appreciates it. However, active listening may also entail the transformation of the speaker's ideas into a form that the listener can understand. For example, during a political debate, if one person is discussing taxes and another is discussing welfare, it would be beneficial for both to hear how their points might fit together when viewed in the context of the whole.

The listener may also express agreement, disagreement, or support in response to the message. These responses contribute to the sense of shared understanding and give the speaker the impression that their ideas are being heard.

The advantages of active listening extend not only to the speaker but also to the listener. The listener can receive and comprehend ideas that would otherwise go unnoticed or be misunderstood. They also gain a better understanding of the perspectives of others.

Common listening issues and how to solve them
Active listening is a communication technique in which the listener participates actively and constructively by asking questions and providing feedback. Active listening, as opposed to passive listening, in which the listener occasionally nods or says "I see" but does not contribute much to the conversation, requires both partners to be engaged.

The following are some common listening issues and how to solve them:

A. **Defensiveness** - The inability to listen to criticism in a nonjudgmental, open-minded manner. This is treated by becoming aware of one's behaviors and how they affect others. Being mindful is the most effective way to become more aware.

B. **Boredom** - Creates the impression that the speaker's words are unimportant. This is remedied by asking the speaker to elaborate on ideas from a different and more in-depth perspective.

C. **Answering before listening** - During the presentation, answers questions and/or make statements that are not reflective of what was said. This is remedied by asking pertinent questions and requesting clarification when necessary.

D. **Attacking the speaker** – Making disparaging remarks about the speaker's presentation, often in a superior tone. This is remedied by making small comments that assist the speaker in understanding and adapting their approach in some way.

E. **Asking unnecessary questions** – Taking a listener's point, but then questioning it further. This can be avoided by only asking questions about the topic at hand.

F. **Distracting** – Often victims of their misunderstandings, do not actively listen to the speaker and interrupt them. This is remedied by making a concerted effort to comprehend what the speaker is saying.

G. **Guilt** – When a person feels guilty for not listening and apologizes, the "I'm terrible" or "I didn't listen" syndrome occurs. This is remedied by forgiving yourself and moving forward.

Instructions for repairing common hearing problems:

1. **Awareness** – Be aware of how you listen and your physical and emotional reactions to what others say. For example, if you are tired, you may fall asleep during the presentation. Knowing when this is likely and when you should stay awake will help you improve your active listening skills.

2. **Empathy** – Listening patterns are primarily based on

emotions, how people perceive themselves, what they want from others, and how they want others to perceive them. Utilize these emotions to comprehend why other people's words or actions are inappropriate. The more you can empathize with what others are trying to say, the better you will understand what they are saying.

3. **Participation** – Active listening necessitates the listener to contribute ideas, ask questions, and seek clarification as needed.

4. **Assertiveness** – You can express interest in what was said without dismissing the speaker. Being assertive entails considering the purpose of your listening rather than simply blocking out everything around you and focusing your entire attention on what is being said.

5. **Listening consists of two steps**: You hear first, then you listen. The first step is to collect information. Pay attention to everything the speaker says. Many people, for example, appear to lose track of what they're saying in order not to forget anything, and as a result, they repeat themselves or become stuck in one area of conversation.

6. **Feedback** – Active listeners actively participate in the conversation by expressing interest in what has been said and asking for clarification when necessary.

7. **Response** – As you listen, consider how you will respond to what is said. Not only does this demonstrate interest, but it also allows you to clarify and follow up on the topic at hand, or it introduces a new topic of conversation.

8. **Connect** – The next time you listen, look for something that relates what you heard to something else you know. It could be a similar situation, a person or place, or the story's emotional impact. This is where active listening transforms into interaction rather than passive hearing.

These simple tips for active listening are effective and can make a difference in whether or not your conversation is productive. That's something to keep an eye on!

CHAPTER 5
EMPATHIC DIALOGUE

Empathic dialogue is characterized by two people conversing in such a way that they attempt to understand each other's thoughts and feelings.

These emotions could be related to a specific topic or to something that happened recently to either individual.

The key component of empathic dialogue is that both parties actively listen to one another before weighing their responses. When you begin to empathize, you will quickly learn to listen to the other person's message and respond appropriately.

Empathic dialogue is critical in the development of stronger relationships. It is a method of listening with more than just your ears; you listen with your heart and mind as well. Empathy allows people to connect on a much deeper level with one another and can help to create the conditions for great things to happen.

Empathic communication facilitates a more meaningful relationship. Individuals are more open to hearing and seeing in the same way when they believe they are being seen and heard. Even if they do not agree, that connection can help both sides understand each other. Compromise becomes much easier as a result of this understanding, allowing for greater progress on the issue at hand rather than a difference of opinion.

Empathic dialogue is similar to active listening, but it goes a step further. It necessitates that an individual not only listens to the other person's point of view with an open mind but also feels what the other person feels. When someone can offer you empathic dialogue, they can put themselves in your shoes and understand why you feel the way you do and what brought you to this point.

Empathic dialogue is a type of communication in which the other person's needs are met in their current state. When someone listens with empathy, they gain a better understanding of what makes them anxious or overwhelmed. They can respond to your emotions, and their responses will be more effective if they have considered what you truly want to hear. An empathic dialogue partner can assist you in reframing your perspective, becoming aware of your own emotions, and confronting your issues. When you find a partner who can listen to you with empathy, you will be able to have more effective and thoughtful conversations that will lead to common goals and outcomes.

When you want to know how someone feels or why they believe they are correct, use active listening? Active listening can be used to understand how someone is feeling or what problems they are having in an empathic manner. To empathically communicate, one must actively listen to understand what the speaker is saying. To empathically listen, you must try to put yourself in the shoes of the other person and understand their meaning and intentions. You must be sympathetic and caring.

Self-awareness grows as a result of empathic dialogue. It fosters personal growth and fosters trust between two parties. When attempting to identify problems in a collaborative setting, many people focus on the relationship level. It can assist participants in focusing on their internal issues.

Empathetic dialogue can also help you identify your internal messages. It allows you to put yourself in the shoes of another person by hearing and comprehending how he or she feels. To achieve the ultimate goal of empathically grasping the other person's perspective, the individual must be able to accurately reflect their feelings. The emotional level of this interaction is reflected in this reflection. You must conduct preliminary research to reflect. To reflect, the individual must learn about the other person's problems and the solutions they propose.

Empathetic dialogue can assist an individual in improving team communication. It encourages participants to confront their issues, which can lead to positive outcomes. This dialogue enables groups to look beyond their problems and learn from the experiences of others.

Empathic listening entails more than just the listener's ability to hear the needs of others. It also includes a willingness to reflect on another person's feelings, which includes a curious attitude, expressing what you feel, and expressing what you receive from the other person.

Empathically listening necessitates considering and attempting to understand the other person's feelings, thoughts, and motives.

Empathic listening is concerned with the other person's point of view, how they are feeling, how they are thinking, and what they would like to happen. The goal is not to enable, but to understand. It's not about you; it's about them. It's about the other person and what they're going through at the time. It facilitates communication between people by improving their understanding of each other's points of view, allowing them to better understand each other.

The ability to listen with empathy is a valuable skill that can be developed in a variety of ways. Empathic listening entails focusing on the speaker's emotions and needs rather than the message itself. Empathic listening involves reflecting the listener what he or she has said, using phrases such as "I see, I feel."

There are also various types of empathy. Personal empathy is one type. This is when a person empathizes with another person they know personally and feels similar emotions to what the other person is feeling. The individual may be able to relate on a deeply personal level, or they may have had a similar experience in the past. This is also known as "emotional empathy." Cognitive empathy is the second type of empathy. This is when a person understands the feelings and emotions of another person but does not necessarily feel or experience the same feelings or emotions. Cognitive empathy is defined as "considering" the other person's situation. "Emotional contagion" is the third type of empathy. This happens when an individual's emotions and mood are influenced by the emotions and moods of others.

The three types of empathy have varying degrees of intensity. "Sympathetic concern" is the highest level of empathy. This entails feeling bad when someone else is feeling bad. It entails wanting to assist another person by comforting them and doing something to make them feel better. The second level of empathy is referred to as "personal distress."

This happens when one person feels bad but not as bad as the other person. They are more concerned with their feelings than with the feelings of others. The lowest level of empathy is referred to as "social facilitation." When an individual feels good when someone else feels good, this is referred to as social facilitation. Social facilitation can be beneficial or detrimental. It can be considered positive if it makes the other person feel better and negative if it is used to make the other person feel bad.

Listen, Reflect, Acknowledge, Ask Questions, Paraphrase/Reflect, and Summarize are the steps for empathic dialogue.

1. **Paying Attention**
   Listening entails hearing what the other person is saying and concentrating on the meaning of what they are saying. It entails comprehending their mindset, feelings, and emotions. It necessitates your willingness to hear and reflect on what the other person has said.

2. **Think about it**
   Reflecting is effectively putting yourself in the shoes of another person and attempting to comprehend his or her point of view as they perceive it. It may entail paraphrasing what they said to demonstrate that you have heard them and are empathizing. Understanding the emotions and attitudes underlying what they are saying is part of reflecting.

3. **Recognition**
   Acknowledging means responding in a way that shows you understand and empathize with what they're saying. It clarifies what was previously said, allowing the other person to focus on the current situation and allow them to express their feelings more easily and effectively.

4. **Pose inquiries**
   Some people may be unable to express themselves or may not feel comfortable doing so, and they may lack communication skills. They may be unsure of how they feel or what they require, which can cause them to appear angry or upset when they are, in fact, shy or nervous. An empathic question can assist the other person in expressing their concerns.

5. Reflect/Reflect back

Saying what you heard in your own words is what paraphrasing is.

This allows you to respond to what they have said. It is beneficial for the other person to know that you heard and comprehended what they were saying.

6. Recapitulate

The final step is to recall everything you've learned about the person and what they've said. It also aids in documenting everyone's feelings, both now and throughout the discussion.

Empathic dialogue between groups can help improve communication skills by using empathy as a problem-solving tool in group situations. Empathic dialogue is beneficial to groups because it teaches members how to use empathy effectively to solve problems and communicate with one another. It can be used as a team-building tool for any group or organization that wants to improve communication or lead with more empathy.

CHAPTER 6
MANAGEMENT OF FEEDBACK IN COMMUNICATION

When dealing with another person, feedback can be used to help get to the bottom of a problem. This type of feedback is referred to as active listening, and it is extremely effective in promoting healthy communication within an organization. Active listening is the process of receiving feedback, whether positive or negative, and devoting time to considering the message before responding to it.

A person can receive and analyze feedback more objectively if they choose not to react immediately. By providing a well-thought-out response, the person is internally considering what they can do better in the future without becoming defensive and attempting to justify their actions. The main goal of active listening is to improve as a person by learning from feedback. This type of feedback is most effective when it is constructive and people are willing to accept that they will need to change certain aspects of their behavior.

Active listening can also help to foster a better communication environment within an organization. When managers receive feedback, they can become more aware of how their employees feel about the quality of their work and their needs as individuals. This awareness can lead to a work environment in which employees feel more valued and, as a result, have a stronger sense of loyalty to the company. Furthermore, feedback allows managers to get to know their employees on a more personal level.

Because feedback is so important in improving communication, it should be implemented regularly within an organization. This would allow people to concentrate on how they could improve their behavior and perform better. Feedback isn't always easy, but it can be extremely beneficial to both parties. A more personalized communication process and a more loyal employee base benefit the organization. Employees benefit from a workplace that values them as individuals, supports them, and encourages them to grow.

The goal of feedback is to assist in identifying and resolving problems within an organization. When evaluating an employee's level of quality in a given situation, it's critical to provide honest feedback. To make the process more effective, start with praise when appropriate. Following that, things can be nitpicked or discussed as needed. People are more likely to have constructive conversations if they begin with praise and then leave the room on good terms.

Being open about one's own needs and feelings is the best way to get quality feedback. As a result, the employee will feel more at ease providing honest feedback in return. This openness also aids in the development of a positive relationship with a manager.

The feedback process provides a unique opportunity for managers and employees to become closer as individuals and to build trust within an organization. Even if the information is negative, it can still help deal with a problem or situation. People can feel more at ease sharing their emotions if you are thorough and ask open-ended questions. The goal of providing feedback is to make people feel good about the situation while also helping them improve as individuals.

You can have more influence on the outcome of a situation or problem if you express yourself more effectively. This type of feedback aids in the development of a better work environment, the development of employee loyalty, and the development of communication skills within an organization.

When receiving feedback, it is important to listen carefully and actively. Common responses such as "That's not true" should be avoided. This is referred to as defensiveness because instead of accepting feedback and considering ways to improve their communication, they are justifying or explaining why something isn't true. Instead of attempting to be the smarter person, they demonstrate their intelligence at the expense of others.

Accepting feedback and being open-minded about how a person could have done things differently is sometimes the best way to improve communication. Thanking someone for their time and considering how the situation could have been handled differently is a more effective way to receive feedback.

Managers can use feedback to improve organizational communication. This may result in improved employee relationships, increased respect from coworkers, and increased efficiency. Employees should be open-minded and avoid becoming defensive when receiving feedback from a manager. In the long run, this can lead to better company culture and higher employee performance.

CHAPTER 7:
BREAKING DOWN
COMMUNICATION BARRIERS

People frequently have difficulty communicating with one another. They don't want to, but they find it difficult to express themselves or even ask for what they want. People will usually try to figure out what the other person wants by interpreting their body language and facial expressions. This is acceptable, and it works the majority of the time. However, there are times when you simply want to be direct and say what you want without having to go through all of that trouble.

In any type of relationship, clear communication is essential. We can't have a good relationship, a good team effort, or even a normal conversation with someone if we can't understand them.

By learning how to actively listen, you will be able to break down any communication barriers. Don't talk when someone else is talking. Don't try to anticipate what they'll say next. Simply listen to them out and then respond when they're finished. This is active listening, and it is how you should communicate if you want your relationship or team effort to succeed.

Communication is essential in any type of relationship, platonic or romantic. There may be times when one person prefers to do things one way while the other prefers to do things another way. That's when you have to communicate with each other to figure out which path is best. You can't always expect them to do things your way. When it comes to communication, you may have to compromise and let them have their way. Everyone should be able to communicate effectively with one another, and then everything should go smoothly from there. This way, you can have a fun relationship while also working effectively as a team.

These pointers may help you understand how to improve communication:

Listen to what the other person has to say for a while. If you're having difficulty with this, you should try practicing your communication skills with someone you know.

Don't be afraid to ask questions or make requests of the other person. However, make certain that you do so at the appropriate time. Make sure it's at a convenient time for both of you so that you can both listen attentively and respond appropriately.

Always respond to questions promptly. If you find yourself in a situation where you are unable to respond, it is best to apologize and let the other person know that you will be able to respond eventually.

Never be afraid to clarify your points. It can be extremely beneficial to ask the other person for an explanation or clarification of what they're attempting to say. If you do so assertively but courteously, they are more likely to respond appropriately.

If you want to change the subject of a conversation, it's best to do so directly. It's never a good idea to try to change the subject by avoiding it or steering the conversation in a different direction. You'll be much more successful in shifting the topic of discussion if you're assertive and open about your intentions.

Finally, when it's time to end your conversation, it's best to do so politely and cordially. You won't leave the person with a negative impression of you if you do it this way.

Don't let communication barriers prevent you from having a meaningful relationship or working effectively as a team. Communicate effectively with one another; this will make your life much easier and more enjoyable.

CHAPTER 8
THE IMPORTANCE OF ACTIVE LISTENING IN WORKPLACE COMMUNICATION

Active listening is a crucial skill to have in the workplace.
Active listening can help you communicate your understanding, increase your understanding, appear more intelligent, and improve your relationships with coworkers and supervisors.

It has also been shown to significantly reduce stress levels in both you and those around you. Active listening is the act of "paying attention" to what someone else is saying in its most basic form. However, there is more to it than that. To be a true active listener, you must not only pay attention but also respond compassionately and effectively to what is said.

There are numerous techniques for practicing active listening, each with its own set of advantages. Active listening can help you learn about your coworkers' backgrounds, feelings, and thoughts, as well as provide ways for you to manage stress with your coworkers.

Active listening in the workplace may result in more effective communication between coworkers and supervisors, allowing them to work more productively together.

Effective communication is regarded as a critical component of establishing, maintaining, and repairing relationships in the workplace.

Improving your communication skills allows you to form new relationships that last after the initial contact. Building a cooperative environment and fostering a positive team mentality can also help you improve relationships with coworkers.

Effective workplace communication can mean the difference between productivity and stagnation. You may discover that your efforts are not well organized as a result of poor communication, resulting in poor productivity. By providing clear and concise explanations and directions, productivity can be increased. Furthermore, a company's overall effectiveness is determined by the collective effectiveness of its employees.

Being an active listener to others can make them feel valued and appreciated. Active listening is effective because it lets people know what you're thinking and helps you maintain a positive attitude toward what they're saying. People also feel more valued and appreciated when their suggestions for improvement are heard and considered. It also aids in the clarification of ideas or concerns that coworkers may have, as well as letting them know that their ideas are being heard. If you listen carefully to your coworkers, they will believe that you are genuinely interested in what they have to say.

Furthermore, active listening demonstrates respect for others in the workplace. When you listen to someone, you are giving that person your complete attention, which shows that you value who he or she is as a person. It also allows people to be themselves without feeling awkward, which contributes to a more relaxed work environment for everyone involved.

Active listening can also help you improve your working relationships with your bosses. You may be better at recognizing your supervisor's concerns and opinions if you listen to him or her. This will allow you to develop a more intimate working relationship. Coworkers may notice a friendly atmosphere in the workplace because disagreements are resolved through honest communication and the importance of listening.

Employees will also be more enthusiastic about their jobs if their suggestions are heard and taken into account. Furthermore, if they believe their ideas are being considered, they will have more confidence in themselves, which will help them provide better quality work.

What Role Does Nonverbal Communication Play in Workplace Communication?

Listening is an important skill that is frequently overlooked in today's competitive work environment. Everyone should be aware of their nonverbal messages, whether in an office meeting, on the phone, or at the water cooler. It's critical to stay motivated and aware of your thoughts and feelings about what you're hearing so that your emotions don't take over. Active listening is the concentrated and disciplined effort to hear, comprehend, accept, and remember what someone has said. After you've listened to someone else's message, it's time for you to respond with your nonverbal cues. When you speak to others, keep in mind that everything you say will be heard through their ears and processed by their brain; as a result, others will be able to read your body language as well.

It is critical to maintaining eye contact while speaking so that others can see that you are paying attention to them. If you don't look at each person when you speak with them, they might think you're uninterested in what they're saying. It's a good idea to look someone in the eyes every time you speak to them; it shows respect and lets them know they're important to you. If you're uncomfortable with that, at the very least focus on a person's eyes and face to demonstrate that you're paying attention to what they're saying. When speaking, a smile can go a long way. Smiles make people feel more relaxed and free when conversing with one another. Avoid crossing your arms or legs while speaking because it conveys that you do not want to be there. It is critical to move so that you do not appear stiff and uncomfortable. To make a good impression on others, it's also a good idea to sit up straight; however, keep your movements small and maneuverable.

Try not to fidget when you're talking to someone. Picking at your clothes, tapping a pencil, or shuffling papers can all be distracting. They will only make the other person feel awkward and self-conscious. Keep your arms by your sides or on the table in front of you while remaining seated. Your body language should always correspond to what you are saying and the message you want to convey to others.

For example, if you "speak" with your hands by keeping them on the table in front of you, it indicates that you are open to what is being said. When you fold your arms over your chest while speaking, others assume you are either not receptive or defensive. In other words, ensure that the nonverbal messages correspond to the verbal messages. Body language is the nonverbal language we use to communicate with others. It doesn't speak, but it tells us a lot about ourselves.

We wouldn't be able to understand people's motivations, emotions, or even the meaning of their words if we didn't have them. Body language may not be written, but that doesn't make it any less important. In some cases, body language communicates more than just a simple feeling or emotion; it sends messages and creates impressions. It's a way for us to express how we feel and think. If you say you're sorry but your body language suggests otherwise, the people around you may not believe you. Many times, our actions match our words; however, there are times when they contradict each other. To be an effective communicator, it is necessary to understand both verbal and nonverbal messages sent and received between people.

You should not be thinking about anything else while listening to others. It is impolite to do so. It conveys to the other person that you are uninterested in what they are saying or that your mind is elsewhere. Concentrate on what they're saying and try to remain calm as they speak. If you can't understand what they're saying, ask them to repeat it. This shows the other person that you are interested in what he or she is saying.

When you make eye contact with someone, it conveys to them that you are interested in what they are saying. It also conveys your interest in what they have to say. Eye contact clearly shows that the other person's thoughts and opinions are important. It demonstrates respect and understanding for the person speaking to you, as well as letting them know that they have your undivided attention.

When you're talking to someone, make an effort to appear interested. This shows the other person that you are interested in what they have to say and that you care about them. It also demonstrates a high level of respect for them and instills confidence in them. Maintain a straight posture and pay close attention. This gives the impression that you are looking out for their best interests and are on their side. This shows that you are trustworthy and dependable, and as a result, more people will want to work with you.

What Successful Leaders Understand About Active Listening and Effective Communication

One of the most important skills in great leadership is the ability to listen. It transforms people into valuable assets and trusted advisers. The ability to communicate, which is the essence of leadership, is a close second to listening. Effective communication with others is often what distinguishes leadership aspirants.

Effective leaders share their vision, take action, and let others know how they can assist. In business, it is often not so much what you say as it is how you say it. How a message is delivered, including tone of voice, timing, and subject matter, is as important as what is said. These factors can determine whether or not a message is received.

Listening is one of the most undervalued skills in effective leadership communication. What distinguishes effective leaders from others? The ability to listen and be open to other people's ideas and thoughts will set you apart from the crowd.

A leader who listens to the opinions and feelings of his employees demonstrates respect for their ideas and can improve his leadership style. A leader who only considers his or her point of view will not achieve the same level of success. A good listener is also a good communicator. A good communicator makes better decisions, acts decisively, and increases productivity.

Communication must be two-way. Listening to what others have to say is always beneficial. Spend time being open to other people's ideas and suggestions. Listening effectively is a skill that can be learned.

Effective communication begins with active listening. Outstanding listening skills result in fewer misunderstandings, less organizational conflict, and increased productivity. Effective communication necessitates the ability to listen compassionately, discern what is important and how best to communicate it, and then convey it clearly and concisely.

Humans have an innate desire to communicate because we want others to understand what we are thinking and feeling. Listen with your heart as well as your head to communicate effectively.

Listening is a two-way street. If you are actively listening—listening to understand, listening to respond, or listening with empathy—you will hear things differently. The quality of your listening will determine how effective you are at communicating. Listening is a skill that should be honed and developed to a high level of proficiency. The more assured you are in your communication abilities, the better you will be able to listen and communicate.

Listening effectively is essential in all aspects of leadership. When you listen to others, you are expressing your interest in their points of view or ideas. When you actively listen to and understand the other person's point of view, you are tacitly accepting that person's right to hold those views. Acceptance fosters trust, which is essential in any interpersonal relationship. People prefer to be heard. When people believe that their opinions have been heard and understood, they will respond more positively when given feedback or direction.

A leader who actively listens, for example, is more likely to have positive relationships with their employees because they demonstrate their interest.

Building rapport is an important part of effective communication. The feeling of trust and sharing that exists between two people is referred to as rapport.

Listening can also help you perform better. The act of listening and learning influences others to work hard to achieve their goals. When you listen, you open yourself up to new, more creative, and inspiring ideas.

Working outside of your comfort zone is a type of leadership. Unconditional support and trust are extremely powerful tools in any leader's arsenal. Leaders who show trust by listening to and supporting others are more confident in their ability to lead their team.

CHAPTER 9
HOW BEING A GOOD LISTENER MAY HELP YOU SUCCEED IN LIFE

It is impossible to achieve success without amassing a wealth of knowledge. You can gain much-needed information from others' experiences and knowledge if you actively listen to them.

Furthermore, you can improve not only as a person but also as a professional.

Nothing is more important than listening to what others have to say, especially when they have something valuable to offer. To be successful, you must be able to recognize potential in others and learn from their experiences. You must pay attention for this process to work.

Learning about successful people will benefit you in both your professional and personal life. You can learn about others and even pick up tips that will help you in your own life if you actively listen.

Active listening is the best way to ensure that you don't miss anything important that someone is saying. It will also assist you in demonstrating respect and interest in what their message may be, as well as demonstrating that you are truly attempting to learn from them. This is an important tool for a professional to have because it can help you assert authority and appear more mature, both of which are important characteristics of a good leader.

When you actively listen, people feel more comfortable opening up to you and sharing their life experiences. Simply by paying attention, you can learn a lot in a short period. By doing so, you will benefit from the knowledge of others and, if necessary, apply it to your own life.

Active listening is the most effective way to boost self-esteem, which is essential for anyone who wants to feel good about themselves and their abilities. When you actively listen, you will gain a better understanding of other people's problems and concerns. If you want to improve your self-esteem and confidence, try active listening and see how much it can help you in your personal and professional relationships.

The importance of active listening cannot be overstated if you want to become more successful in life. It will assist you in better understanding your coworkers and peers, as well as gaining insight into their actions. This is also a great way to connect with those around you.

Active listening can be a valuable tool for both personal and professional growth. You will gain an understanding of others' concerns and goals if you actively listen to them. This will help you understand what they expect from you and the organization as a whole. If you are more engaged with the people around you, you will feel like a better leader and friend. It is also an excellent way to advance in your career.

Active Listening Techniques for Success
Active listening is a skill that allows you to fully comprehend the meanings of others, which is especially useful at work. Active listening can help you make your point in meetings, communicate more effectively with friends and family members, and uncover hidden problems at work.

One of the most common situations in business is when you're in a meeting and you don't understand what they're saying or why they're making certain decisions. Active listening enables you to determine precisely what they mean or why they think and feel the way they do. It can also help you be more effective when presenting your ideas or thoughts because you have taken the time to understand what others are thinking and feeling about your ideas.

And active listening is applicable not only in business situations but also with friends and family. Your friends and family members may be having a problem or require advice that they are not comfortable seeking. You can quickly understand what they are trying to say if you are an active listener.

When it comes to making decisions, you will be more likely to get their buy-in if you listen and truly understand what they are trying to say.

You will be able to make a better impression on your superiors and become a leader within your company if you practice active listening skills in the workplace.

The first step in active listening is to prepare your environment for success. To effectively communicate with others, you must create the right conditions to maximize your understanding and comprehension. To create these conditions, you must first ensure that everyone is at ease enough to open their hearts and minds and share their thoughts.

When you're setting up your environment, make sure that everyone in the room understands why they're there. Explain to them what is going on inside of you and what their role is in the situation. This makes them feel more at ease and secure in sharing their thoughts with you. If they are afraid that something they say will be misconstrued by you, it will be more difficult for them to open up and share their thoughts and feelings.

Make it clear what your goal is for the meeting. Make it clear that the main goal is not to impose your ideas on others, but rather to be open and honest with one another. Being honest with others is an important part of active listening, but saying what you mean can sometimes be misinterpreted as not being honest. To avoid this misunderstanding, whenever possible, explain your reasoning for every action or statement you make in clear terms.

The more open you are about your goals and the more clear you are about everything in your head, the more likely you are to gain confidence and buy-in from others. When you are open, your coworkers will feel safe enough to share their thoughts and ideas, which will lead them to come to you when it is time to share their advice or seek guidance.

If everything goes according to plan, the employees will feel comfortable enough to share their ideas, opinions, and concerns with you. The more you can persuade them to do so, the more likely it is that you will gain their trust and begin to gain their commitment to projects.

The best way to keep people on board with your ideas is to show them that they can rely on you. There is no need for them to be concerned that they will be perceived as a threat or that they will despise you because of who they are or what they believe in. Instead, they will regard you as a supporter and ally.

Remember that how you see yourself is the foundation of being a leader.

To succeed in expanding his vision, a leader must be honest with himself, as well as his ideas and beliefs. In such an environment, you will be able to gain the trust of everyone around you, which will allow you to realize all of your ideas. Be yourself; go above and beyond what others expect of you.

Why Is Being a Good Listener Important in Your Career?

If you want to work in broadcasting, journalism, or the corporate world, you should focus on improving your listening skills. There are numerous opportunities available to listeners who can extract and apply the information correctly! Being able to actively listen is a skill that not everyone possesses and one that you should work hard to improve if you want to be successful in your future career.

Listeners must be able to understand what speakers are saying to comprehend what they require. They should also be able to comprehend the information being presented.

If you want to advance in your career, you must have excellent communication skills. Employers value communication skills because they demonstrate your ability to collaborate with others and assist them. Active listening skills assist you in paying attention and comprehending what is being said. When you can hear what employers have to say, your chances of getting a job or progressing in your chosen career path improve. It is also beneficial when communicating with coworkers.

Listening skills are also necessary for all students and those who want to advance in their careers. This is because it allows them to pick up on what other people are saying and what they are attempting to say. It assists them in understanding the message behind the words being spoken and gives them an idea of what needs to be communicated. It's also important to note that listening makes use of a person's ability to communicate with others in a new way. And, because people work with others all day, listening is an important skill to have. Listening also assists students in gathering information and data for presentations or sharing with others.

Listening is a skill that we are often told as children that we must continue to practice throughout our lives. We've all experienced how aggravating it is when someone isn't paying attention or isn't listening to you. Although learning to listen is important at any age, it can make a significant difference in how well you perform at work or school.

CHAPTER 10
THE IMPORTANCE OF BEING A GOOD LISTENER IN CONVERSATIONS

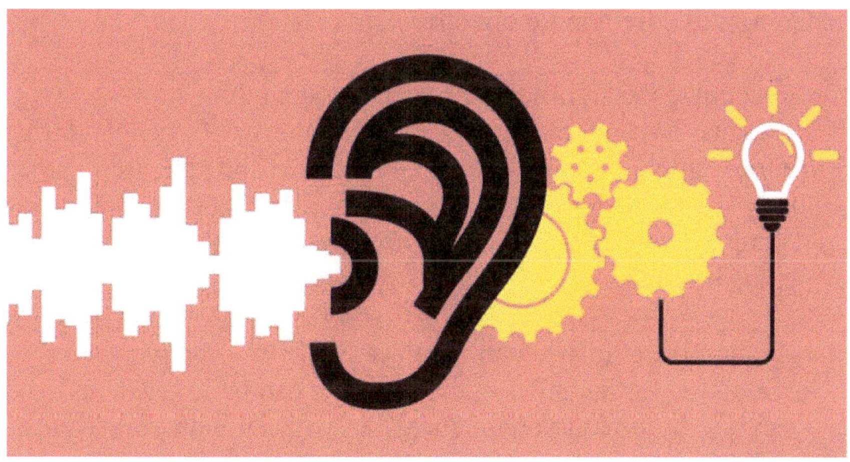

When you're in a meeting or listening to a lecture, you're doing your best to take in as much information as possible. Suddenly, someone asks for your thoughts on the subject, and you're left grasping at straws. When someone starts talking to you, your mind goes blank.

Listening to people and interacting with them is one of the most important aspects of a conversation. Listening is an art that requires great skill and patience, especially when it comes to people whose native language is different from yours. "To listen well," Aristotle once said, "means to hear as the other person sees and hears."

Listening is important not only for improving your understanding of what others say but also for developing confidence.

Being a good listener does not always imply that you are a good talker.

Active listening is a skill that can help you improve the depth and quality of your conversations with others. You gain the patience, tolerance, and confidence to engage in more in-depth and meaningful conversations with others. Listening is not only for people who are talking to you; it should be a habit in your daily life.

Here are some suggestions to help you improve your active listening skills for a more effective conversation:

1. Recognize the significance of active listening
    You can have various types of interactions with people during conversations depending on their reactions and responses. When they are upset, sympathetically talk to them about it. Others feel more at ease and open up to you when you listen calmly and empathically.

2. Acquire the ability to communicate without using words.
    "Don't forget that silence is a skill that can be learned, and you can say more with your silence than you can with your words."
    - Maraboli, Steve
    When it comes to conversations, silence is a very powerful tool. People sometimes need quiet time to think about things and connect what they already know. Encourage them to be silent by remaining silent yourself. Active listening is practiced by repeating what you've heard and making sure that whatever you're saying is not offensive.
    When you are quiet, remember to look at the person who is also quiet.
    People who are introverts and do not easily express their feelings should be treated with caution. Always make an effort to

understand the other person's feelings by clarifying your doubts with open-ended questions such as "how did you feel about that?"

If they say something that comes across as offensive, don't be too quick to respond defensively. Change the subject or simply acknowledge their feelings and explain why you find them offensive. If you do this, you will start a constructive conversation rather than an argument.

Being silent does not imply that you are passive. Constructively resolving conflicts is important in interpersonal relationships because it allows the people communicating to gain a better understanding of each other's feelings and points of view.

3. Don't betray your emotions.

    Even if you are extremely busy, people can be hurt if you appear cold or indifferent. It's always a good idea to be sensitive to other people's feelings and cooperate in small ways, such as talking about your day, making small gestures or saying words that show you care about them, giving frequent compliments, and so on. The less you understand what people are going through, the less you can trust them, and the more likely you are to become superficial with them.

4. Make use of open body language

    Avoid any signs of boredom, such as yawning or tapping your pen or fingers on the table, while listening intently. Use open body language and make eye contact with the other person instead. Keep your arms free and your hands visible so that they can see you are willing to listen to them. The more you use body language, the more confident they will be that you are listening to them.

    By keeping your arms at your sides, you clearly show that you are willing to listen to them. This demonstrates to the other person that you are open and receptive.

5. Don't be overly eager to respond.

    Wait a few seconds before responding instead of responding right away. This will allow you to consider what the other person is saying without reacting too quickly.

6. Ask the appropriate questions
    The right questions can expand your understanding and encourage others to continue talking about a topic you're interested in. Asking questions is a good way to demonstrate your interest in conversing with others and attentively listening.

7. Give your thoughts on what they say.
    When people are speaking, ask them, "How do you feel?" "What happened next?" and "Can you explain more?" It demonstrates your interest in their stories and desires to learn more about what they are saying.

8. Keep a close eye on the person.
    Don't sit too far away from the person or at such a distance that you can't hear what they're saying. When you're listening, make sure your body language and proximity make the other person feel at ease talking with you.

9. Maintain an open mind
    Some of what is said may be difficult to accept or comprehend. If they say something you find incorrect or strange, try not to judge them on it and instead give them the benefit of the doubt by assuming they have a reason for saying what they do.
    Just keep in mind that you should never pass judgment on others based on what they say.

10. Prefer only positive things
    Listening to someone else's story is similar to reading a book. Many of the subtle characteristics associated with their experiences and personality will become apparent to you.

11. Being a good listener entails more than just focusing on what the person is saying to you; it also entails being aware of their body language and other subtle cues they may be giving off.
    Being able to read someone's body language properly will not only help you understand who that person is, but it will also help you remember what they are saying better.

12. Do not pass judgment on the person in question.
It is important to remember that there can be numerous explanations for an action. Sometimes something is simply out of character for a person or does not even fit with their personality, but you are misinterpreting it. People must sometimes do things that they do. The most important thing is to talk to the person about what they're doing and why they're doing it and to understand why they'd do such things in the first place.

13. People express their emotions and feelings in a variety of ways. People's ways of expressing their thoughts and emotions differ from one another. Different things, such as loss, wanting something, needing something, or being happy, can also trigger those emotions. The way people express themselves may also be influenced by the type of relationship they have with the person with whom they are speaking, such as a friend, family member, or coworker. Sometimes a person is unaware of how someone feels in contrast to what they may think or say on the inside, and being aware of this would allow them to fully understand what emotions are being expressed in a conversation.

14. Learn to be vulnerable in front of others.
People will want to talk to you if you talk a lot. People will want to be around you if you listen more.
Keeping your problems and emotions inside is never good for your mental health and well-being. People who are good listeners can inspire others to be good listeners by confiding in them about their feelings and secrets.

15. Speak up when something needs to be said Even if it is tempting to remain silent when your coworkers or manager speak to you, it is best to speak up during a meeting, especially if something is not being addressed.

16. Allow them to feel good about themselves.
Make the other person feel good by letting them know they shared some useful information with you.
You could do this by saying things like "How interesting" or "I had no idea." If they say something useful, let them know by

saying, "Oh, I didn't know that." Please elaborate. "I'm really curious."

If you don't agree with what they're saying, make sure you're not contradicting them by saying things like, "No, I didn't hear that part," or "I'm not sure the writer meant that." The other person will feel better about themselves and be more likely to talk if you are open and receptive.

17. Pay attention without agreeing or disagreeing
This is an important aspect of listening as well. You must listen to what is being said without agreeing or disagreeing with it. This keeps the lines of communication open and the conversation flowing.
So don't respond with "I agree" or "That's correct." Don't try to justify what they've said by saying things like, "I thought you meant something completely different." I had no idea how difficult that must have been for you." Instead, give them a 'pass' and wait for them to finish their sentence.

18. Be present in the moment
Staying in the moment is a good way to achieve effective listening. It is critical not to allow other things to distract you while you are listening. This includes reading documents on your computer, conversing with others and even watching television.

When you are listening, you must be present and attentive to what they are saying. Maintain eye contact and fully focus on what they are saying rather than checking up on other things you are doing.

Allow people time to speak to make it easier for them to speak freely.

Tell them you'll listen intently for as long as they need to speak. They will have your undivided attention and will be more willing to share information with you as a result.

How Active Listening Can Help You Live a Better Life

This is a simple, easy technique that will change your life.

All that is required is a little understanding and the willingness to listen to the other person. We're conditioned as a society to talk in ways where one party is always talking and the other listener is just waiting for their turn. As a result, conversations can be exhausting, and it's difficult to learn anything new because people will only tell you what they already know. You'll miss out on potentially life-altering conversations! It all starts with better listening, but you'll have to force yourself to do it if you want to have an amazing experience.

Everything will change if you can listen. You'll be able to learn new things, positively influence others, and, ultimately, have an impact on the world around you. There are numerous ways in which listening can improve your life:

1. You can alter people's perceptions of themselves.
    When people talk about themselves, they frequently use a negative tone. That is something you can change! All you have to do is listen to them objectively and pay close attention to them. People feel better about themselves when you listen to them. Everyone appreciates someone who listens to them and gives them their full attention.

2. You will be able to significantly assist people.
    Most people are unaware of how their words affect others. They say things that hurt others, even if they don't mean to, but it's a big deal to the person who is hurt. Listening allows you to understand how someone is feeling and how you can assist them. You can learn things about people that will make them feel better about themselves. You may also learn about issues that are bothering them and how you can assist them.

3. You can discover more about yourself.
    Listening is the most effective way to discover your motivations and desires. When you take a step back and focus on how

someone feels, what they want, and what possible solutions are available to them, you can better understand yourself. Understanding begins to come naturally when you focus on this type of listening. The more people you listen to in this manner, the better off you will be.

4. You'll be able to listen to people who speak different dialects more effectively.
    Your understanding will improve if you listen for the same things in everyone. This means you'll be able to hear people who speak differently than you. You'll also be better able to understand people who have a habit of not finishing their sentences or who use fillers like "um," "like," and so on.

The only way to improve your understanding is to improve your listening skills.

You will become a better listener as you practice these skills. You'll develop good listening habits, and understanding what others are saying will become second nature. Keep in mind that many of these things require time and practice to master. Begin small and work your way up; it is entirely possible!

CHAPTER 11
ACTIVE LISTENING TECHNIQUES

Active listening is a skill that you must master, and it is one of the most important skills to cultivate as an effective communicator.

This is because active listening is fundamentally about taking the time to hear what someone else is saying. You pay attention to what they say and how they say it, rather than simply responding or reacting in kind. This allows you to not only engage your conversation partner more meaningfully but also to focus on what is most important at the time.

Here are some active listening techniques to consider:

1. Thank your listener.

Pay attention to how someone says something when you're listening to them. Is their demeanor upbeat? Are there any words that they keep repeating or that they may rephrase? Is it obvious what they're trying to say? It's critical to keep your understanding of what the other person is attempting to describe in mind while actively listening.

2. Avoid interruptions.

Listening without interrupting is one of the most important aspects of active listening. A good way to accomplish this is to pause for a moment before responding. This allows you to process what you've just heard and determine whether or not your response will be helpful. As you might expect, bombarding someone who is talking with questions about the details they've just been given isn't always helpful.

3. Concentrate on the words

A great example of this type of active listening is when you are completely focused on someone's words and only their words – without thinking about how you will respond. Don't try to fill in the blanks or cherry-pick information that makes sense in your head. Instead of being distracted by your thoughts, listen carefully and completely to the listening process.

4. Be aware of your body language

This is an important aspect of active listening. You can show that you are paying attention by nodding, leaning forward slightly, making eye contact (without staring), and even mirroring their posture or facial expressions. The speaker will feel more heard and understood as a result of this. Mirroring the other person's body language is especially important when trying to establish rapport with them, but it's also useful in making the person you're speaking with feel like you're taking them seriously and reflecting on what they've just said.

5. Write a summary of what you've heard.

When active listening, one final technique is to summarize what you've just heard. When dealing with a complex conversation, it's an especially useful way to ensure that both parties understand what the other considers important. It can also be a good way to identify any misconceptions or misunderstandings that may have occurred during the conversation, and it can provide an opportunity for both parties to clarify their understanding of the situation, whatever it may be.

6. Exhibit empathy

This is a great way to demonstrate that you've "heard" someone, but it's also extremely important. When you interact with others or share your ideas, you want them to feel confident that you are concerned about their well-being. Part of this entails being able to understand and empathize with them, which entails not only really listening to what they're saying but also giving them the impression that you understand how your words will impact their struggles ethically.

7. Be genuine and authentic.

You can't fake it when it comes to listening. This means that when you interact with others, you must be yourself. You must be able to relax and not worry about putting on an act, instead of focusing on truly understanding what the other person is saying. Furthermore, this entails being clear about your own opinions and ensuring that your ideas can be traced back to your own experiences or feelings.

8. Be patient.

It's easy to get caught up in your own emotions and lose sight of what's important, especially when trying to communicate in an argument. That's why patience is so important: if you can keep your cool and focus on what the other person is saying, you can avoid becoming distracted by the intense emotions that frequently arise during the heated debate.

9. Display alert body language

There are numerous nonverbal communication methods. One method is to use your body language. Leaning forward and making attentive facial expressions, for example, can make others feel more at ease in a conversation. This kind of attentive body language is important because it shows that you are genuinely interested in what the other person is saying.

10. Pay attention to how others listen.

When you want to improve your listening skills, one of the best ways to do so is to observe how others listen. When you're conversing with others, try to pay attention to how they process information. Do they actively or passively listen? Are they skilled at asking pertinent follow-up questions? Paying attention to how others listen allows you to identify aspects of their behavior that you want to emulate.

11. Practicing

To improve your ability to listen well, you must do more than just devise a strategy and then go through the motions. Instead, you should practice active and engaged listening.

12. Have the fortitude to listen intently.

When it comes to improving your listening skills, being willing to hear what others have to say goes hand in hand with being able to hear when they are not interested in sharing their thoughts.

Someone who dares to truly listen and understand another person's point of view will benefit greatly from deep listening – and will be a valuable asset to any team whose goal is to make better decisions as a group.

Active listening is a useful technique, but it does require some practice. In the end, it's all about making others feel heard, which makes people more willing to share their thoughts and ideas with you. As a result, you will be able to understand what people are thinking better than anyone else, and you will be able to develop stronger relationships.

CHAPTER 12: IMPROVING YOUR RELATIONSHIPS THROUGH ACTIVE LISTENING

Listening is the most effective way to make someone feel appreciated.

Active listening entails tuning out what you believe the other person is saying and concentrating on their emotions and thoughts. This kind of listening will make your partner feel more supported, understood, and validated. Because of the increased emotional connection, a supportive partner can have a positive impact on your mental health. Dealing with problems and emotions is a natural part of life. A better understanding of our own emotions, as well as the emotions of our family and friends, may aid in the discovery of solutions that work for both of us. You can learn to listen in a supportive, respectful manner that makes your partner feel heard and understood. When you actively listen, you will begin to see the world through the eyes of your partner. This contributes to a deeper level of communication in your relationship. You'll start to feel more connected, and the advantages may extend beyond your personal life.

Active listening allows you to empathize with others, which can help you deal with them more effectively. Your ability to understand emotions and remain calm in a crisis will help you deal with stress better than someone who struggles to listen. Constructive communication can aid in the reduction of unhealthy stress reactions. A greater ability to cope with stress can be beneficial to your mental health. It may assist you in maintaining a positive attitude and overall emotional well-being.

Active listening is a way of listening without judging, without offering advice, and without feeling compelled to intervene. Sometimes we are so overwhelmed by our emotions that we want to solve the problem right away. Active listening enables us to slow down and be completely present at the moment. It enables us to understand what our partner is going through. This will assist us in comprehending their concerns and feelings. The simple act of listening can have a significant impact on someone's life. Simultaneously, active listening has been shown to improve your relationship and overall mental health. It will allow you to express yourself more effectively, think more clearly, and feel more connected to others. The advantages are obvious, and there are numerous ways to begin practicing active listening.

This is especially important if you're in a relationship because, in many cases, we don't get enough time or attention from our partners. So, if you can improve your listening skills, your partner will feel more valued and loved.

As you are aware, listening is not as simple as it appears. We sometimes tune out what the other person is saying and simply wait for our turn to speak. We say we're listening, but we're thinking about what we're going to say next to our partner. Others struggle to focus on something else while their partner speaks. All of these are indications of ineffective listening. Your partner will feel heard and valued if you know how to listen effectively. They will have more faith in your emotional connection.

Here are some easy ways to improve your listening skills:

1. Pay close attention and listen carefully. Make an effort to listen to what your partner is saying rather than simply nodding or stumbling over words.
   Allow them to speak and be patient with their speaking style. Interrupting or speaking before they finish makes them feel as if they haven't been heard.

2. Maintain eye contact while listening or speaking. We don't always make eye contact. This could be due to distraction or a lack of comfort with the situation. If you want to connect with your partner, look them in the eyes and show them that you are interested in what they are saying. Don't make them feel uncomfortable by staring at them, but give them your undivided attention.

3. Demonstrate that you're paying attention by asking questions. This will allow you to have a more effective conversation with your partner and demonstrate to them that you are interested in what they are saying. For them to share more information with you, ask open-ended questions. When they have finished speaking, acknowledge what they have said.

4. When speaking with your partner, keep your mind on the present moment. This will make them feel more at ease and will allow you to connect more deeply. Because their emotions are important, try focusing on what they're feeling rather than the past or future.
   For example, if your partner is discussing a past issue, try to connect with the emotions that they are currently experiencing. Say something like, "I know you're still angry about what happened three years ago," to remind yourself of this.

5. Don't chastise your partner if they make a mistake.
   Instead, simply acknowledge that they made a mistake and put them at ease about it.

6. Never correct your partner in front of others. Keep it between the two of you, no matter how uncomfortable you are.

7. Never, ever tell someone they're wrong just to make yourself feel better!
   Our partners may see things differently than we do, and they may be correct. Accept and learn to appreciate your differences!

8. Don't feel obligated to offer your opinion unless they specifically request it. Let them know you're interested in what they have to say and that you'd like to hear more of their ideas.

9. If you are concerned that you will say something that will upset your partner, wait until they have finished their conversation.
   It can be difficult to tell when other people want us to be quiet, but remember that what they say is their business and theirs alone. Be prepared to respect their privacy.

10. If your partner is saying something that makes you uncomfortable, use tactful language to let them know you are still listening.

11. If you're at a loss for words, try saying "I don't know" or "I'm sorry."

12. Acknowledge your frustration with what your partner is saying! It's perfectly normal to feel this way in certain circumstances! The key is to avoid putting them down or making them feel bad about themselves.

Active listening in a relationship is a difficult but rewarding task. If your partner is difficult to listen to or communicate with, your relationship may feel superficial and shallow. Learning to listen effectively will result in a more secure connection in your relationship.

It's not just about how the speaker can be more sensitive, empathic, and responsive; it's also about how the listener can be more sensitive, empathic, and responsive. It is a skill that requires time and practice.

How Being a Good Listener Can Help You Improve Your Relationships

Active listening is a skill that improves our relationships with others.

Good communication is the foundation of all relationships, and being an attentive listener will aid in the development of trust and encourage others to open up.

Active listening shows respect, gives the speaker a sense of importance and shows that you've been paying attention. It's a powerful way to acknowledge another person's thoughts and feelings; if done correctly, it will make those around you feel respected and appreciated.

Here are seven reasons why listening is so important in a relationship:

Respect is demonstrated by listening. When you actively listen, you demonstrate to others that you value their ideas and opinions. They will be more open to ideas and suggestions if they believe they have been heard.

Significant ideas are being heard. Listening allows people to concentrate on what is important and encourages them to prioritize their work. It enables them to clearly express their needs and desires. It also allows them to hear your suggestions and feedback.

Listening allows you to learn more about others: The more you pay attention to others, the better you will understand them. Active listening communicates to others that they are important to you. This is an excellent tool for obtaining what you want from others.

It responds to their needs and acknowledges their significance. People frequently feel unimportant when they are not listened to. Listening shows that you respect and value their opinion. It communicates to them that their needs are important and valid.

It gets you ready for what's to come. If you listen to others, you'll notice what they like and dislike, allowing you to plan for what they might or want next. It also communicates to people that their thoughts and feelings are valued.

It allows you to better understand others. The most obvious way to understand what someone is saying is to listen. You'll be able to learn about what they value most in life and what their needs are by actively listening.

Listeners are more memorable. People who hear you will remember your interest and attention. It can make them feel good and help you establish a reputation as a thoughtful person.

People enjoy being heard because it makes them feel important.

They'll appreciate and respect your enthusiasm. The more they trust you, the better they will work with you and listen to your ideas.

Active Listening in Relationships is a skill that should be practiced.

Personal communication with others is essential for all types of relationships, from friends to romantic partners.

Individuals who lack interpersonal skills are unable to be empathetic toward a listener or hold meaningful conversations. Here's where active listening comes into play. On average, people only listen to about 10% of what is said. This leads to a lack of understanding of a wide range of topics, from the serious to the trivial.

Potential partners usually spend time together doing things that require a lot of communication, such as eating out or going to activities. It is even more important to pay attention to what the other person is saying in these situations. People who actively listen are more likely to have a successful relationship because they demonstrate that they are truly listening and caring, which is the foundation of any good relationship.

Active listening is a highly effective skill that can be applied in a variety of contexts and situations. Here are four simple examples of this skill in use. To practice active listening, simply follow these simple steps:

1. Pay complete and undivided attention to the people with whom you are conversing.
2. Reiterate what that person has said by repeating their words and feelings in different words.
3. Reflect on their emotions to them by repeating what they said but replacing the word "I" with "you." If they say, "I'm very upset about this whole thing," a reflection would be, "It sounds like you're upset about this whole thing."
4. Ask open-ended questions that require a lot of thought and discussion about specific points in the conversation. These kinds of questions allow you to learn more about the other person's worldview.

These simple steps will assist you in improving your interpersonal relationships and communication skills. Remember that active listening fosters intimacy in your relationships and promotes better dialogue so that everyone can better understand each other.

Improve Your Listening and Speaking Skills – Daily Practice

Active listening is essential for developing long-term, trusting relationships with others. It promotes empathy while also increasing self-awareness and clarity in your thoughts and feelings.

Try this practice a few times a day for a week or two and see how it affects your interactions with others:

Amid a conversation, ask yourself, "Am I actively listening or just waiting for my turn to speak?"

If you find yourself listening more than speaking, consider this: "What does that person need to say that is more important than what I need to say?" Make certain that your gestures and facial expressions reflect your beliefs.

If you frequently feel guilty for speaking more slowly than others, it is a good idea to share this with your friends so they can support you in practicing active listening.

Some people rely on their social network to validate their emotions and provide feedback that makes them feel better. This frequently includes seeking reassurance.

When your friends notice that you aren't listening as much as they would like, they may be less willing to respond as quickly or openly. This can make you feel as if you're not connecting with them.

If this occurs, ask yourself, "What can I do to demonstrate to my friends that I am paying attention?"

It is always a good idea to prepare for conversations by considering what your friend may need to share and how you might respond in ways that feel genuine to you.

Ask yourself each time you engage in active listening, "Did my friend feel supported by the way I responded?" If that doesn't work, try again. It may take some time to master this skill.

When you can actively listen with a clear awareness of what the other person may need, you are much less likely to react negatively if someone else responds unexpectedly.

Some people have reported that their friends and family members were irritated when they expressed their thoughts on the situation.

If this happens to you, remind yourself that your opinions are not based on a complete understanding of the situation. Your friends and family should be proud of your efforts to be productive.

The more we practice active listening, the more open we are to new information from others.

We are less likely to react negatively or dismissively when others say what they need to say because we know they are simply trying to share their ideas with us.

Even if you are not directly involved in the topic, try to practice active listening. This will make you feel more connected to others and will allow you to strengthen your bonds with those in your network.

If this is a new experience for you, it may take some time for old habits to fade. It is a good idea to develop new habits that will help you succeed.

Consider new approaches to listening when brainstorming ways to improve relationships in your life. Your relationships will improve as you practice active listening. The happier you are, the better your relationships are.

If you're having trouble with this, a good technique is to ask someone you trust how they would react in the same situation, and then practice how you might react.

Because of your improved active listening skills, your relationships with others will become smoother and more enjoyable over time.

CHAPTER 13
THE SECRET OF SUCCESSFUL PEOPLE

The ability to listen is essential for success. It may appear mundane and overly simple, but it is one of the most important traits to cultivate on your path to success. Listening does not simply entail hearing what is being said; it also entails actively listening, which entails making an effort to understand someone else's story or point of view. It is critical that you can tell when someone is attempting to reach out to you or when they are providing feedback.

People will talk around you, but if you listen carefully, you will hear the most important thing that needs to be said.

One of the most valuable skills, especially in a business meeting, is the ability to separate what people say for the sake of saying something from what is meaningful; this alone requires skill and an active decision on your part. It's no coincidence that the most successful people are also the best listeners.

You must also be able to listen to yourself and your intuition and act on it. You've been told to follow your dreams and what you believe is right since you were a child, and if you ignore your gut feeling in favor of taking the path of least resistance, you may lose sight of what is truly important.

Listening is a skill that can be honed with practice and will help you excel in any field. People who can listen are the most successful in life because they possess the qualities required to be a good leader, a good son or daughter, and even a good friend. You will learn what works for you and what does not by being able to listen to other people's ideas and opinions. You may also gain an understanding of how people act in different situations. When it comes to understanding why some people succeed while others fail, the difference is always in listening and reacting.

You can't act unless you can first listen.

You will never understand what is important to someone if you do not know how to listen to them. They may not even be aware of it, but if you pay close attention, you will be able to figure it out by picking up on cues that are not even verbalized.

You can also teach others how to listen more effectively by demonstrating good and bad practices. It's a skill that can be used in both directions. That's important because if you're giving as well as receiving, you'll have the chance to learn something new, which you can then apply to your situation.

Conclusion

Active listening is a fundamental communication technique.

It makes no difference what the topic of the discussion is; it is critical to actively listen. That is a technique that can be used in a variety of situations.

Active listening can also aid in the information-gathering process.

This is because when you are actively listening, you are more likely to remember both the message and how it made you feel. When you use active listening correctly, you are more likely to obtain information that can be applied in a variety of situations.

Active listening necessitates that the listener hears everything that is said accurately, without passing judgment or adding anything of one's own to what is heard. Active listening aims to elicit an empathic response and make the other person feel understood. In this sense, active listening is an important relationship skill for building trust and encouraging partners to be more open.

Active listening is also an important skill for all managers to have. It is a method of managing and resolving conflict. When active listening is used in conflict situations, it can improve working relationships and increase organizational productivity. Communication, including active listening, is critical in resolving conflicts and building effective teams.

When a listener is actively listening, they are paying attention to the speaker, understanding and demonstrating that they have heard what is being said. It necessitates that the listener is prepared to pause, listen intently, and respond empathically. The active listener can be viewed as a communication facilitator because he or she creates an environment in which people feel free to express their feelings and ideas.

According to a more recent interpretation of active listening, the active listener should not only demonstrate understanding and pay attention to what the speaker is saying, but also accept their point of view. This means that if someone expresses an opinion that is opposed to yours and you do not accept that opinion as valid, you do not fully comprehend what they are attempting to convey. In other words, a person can listen actively while rejecting what is being said – or appear to listen actively while rejecting the speaker's point of view entirely.

Active listening can take many different forms. The most common type seen in the workplace is "active reflection." This type of active listening focuses on the speaker and what they are saying, but it also includes listener reflection. Reflective listening encourages the listener to consider their feelings and ideas as they listen.

Active listening helps people connect. It's a way of expressing your interest in someone and what they're saying.

There is no connection when the listener is not engaged in active listening, which can be detrimental to an organization's culture.

Several studies have found that active listening "increases employee satisfaction and decreases turnover." This creates an environment in which it is much easier to collaborate as a team and resolve conflict.

It also enables effective communication when delegating responsibilities or tasks to other employees. In other words, you can make them aware of your expectations and ensure that they understand what they need to do.

Active listening can help you in a variety of situations. For example, if you are a manager, it will help your employees feel valued in terms of their opinions and ideas. If you are a parent and your child expresses an idea or emotion to you, active listening will help the child feel heard and accepted. It may also strengthen bonds with friends and partners. This is especially important in intimate relationships where the partners need to feel they can trust one another, and it also helps you to be a good leader. It is most helpful when delegating tasks and responsibilities. When someone is actively listening, it conveys the message that they are willing to assist and are getting involved to ensure the project's success.

This can result in a stronger sense of teamwork and unity, which will benefit not only the project but the entire organization!

Active listeners can be successful in a variety of ways. When you are an active listener, more people will feel they can trust you and will be willing to tell you things they would not have told you otherwise. They will also believe they can confide in you about their thoughts, feelings, and problems without fear of being judged. Furthermore, this level of openness and trust makes it easier for them to accept your advice or suggestions.

Active listening is not something that can be learned overnight, but the more you practice it, the better you will become at it. Listening actively takes practice because it requires a conscious effort on your part.

However, the effort is well worth it because active listening facilitates interpersonal communication and increases your chances of success.